RISK TAKERS

STRENGTH

AND

DEVOTION

RISK TAKERS

STRENGTH AND DEVOTION

LINDA FINLAYSON

CF4·K

10 9 8 7 6 5 4 3 2 1
© Copyright 2009 Linda Finlayson
Christian Focus Publications
ISBN: 978-1-84550-492-2
Published by Christian Focus Publications,
Geanies House, Fearn, Tain, Ross-shire,
IV20 1TW, Scotland, U.K.
www.christianfocus.com
email:info@christianfocus.com

Cover design by Daniel van Straaten
Cover illustration by Neil Reed
Printed and bound in Denmark
by Norhaven A/S

For
Irene Ginther,
my Mother

CONTENTS

LET'S GET STARTED

Have you ever looked at a quilt on a bed or hanging on a wall? When you stand back from it, you can see the pattern of the quilt. It could be pictures of flowers, animals or rings all joined together. But when you get closer to the quilt, you can see the pieces that were used to make those bigger pictures. There are lots of different colours and shapes all sewn together. Without those smaller pieces, the quilt would have no pattern at all.

History is a bit like that. When we look back at all the people that lived before us and the things that happened, we can see the pattern of how our country came to be. And then when we look closely at the people's stories who lived back then, we can see all the pieces that came together to make the big pattern.

And so it is with the history of God's kingdom here on earth.

All through the Bible we read about people who either chose to follow God or reject him. We read about the wonderful ways God rescued and helped his people and the great blessings they enjoyed. And that has continued right up until today.

In this book you will read about women who loved God and wanted to serve him even when it became difficult or dangerous. Each of them lived at a different time in history and in different countries. They spoke different languages and dressed in different clothing. But they all had one thing in common. They loved God above all else. They asked God to give them courage and he did.

So come on an adventure. Learn about women who led an army, rescued a baby from death, escaped from a convent, faced a murderous mob, protected a girl from death and climbed mountains all to serve God.

KATHERINE VON BORA

Katherine von Bora lived from 1499–1552 in what we now call Germany. She spent her childhood and early adulthood in a convent. She loved God and felt she could serve him best as a nun. Katherine lived during the time that Dr. Martin Luther had challenged the Roman Catholic Church. He was distressed to see so many people confused by the wrong teaching they received in church and how church leaders tried to tell people they could buy their way into heaven with money and good works. Two years before this story begins, Martin Luther was put on trial for speaking out for God's truth. The judge, Emperor Charles V, excommunicated Martin from the church and he had to go into hiding. From that hiding place, Martin wrote many books and pamphlets to teach people the true doctrines from the Bible. Katherine, living in her convent, came across some of Martin's books and they changed her life. Read on and find out what happened.

ESCAPE!
SPRING 1523

Sister Katherine set the stopper in the clay bottle and wiped the outside with a cloth just as the bell sounded for Vespers. Looking up, she saw Sister Magdalene, her aunt who was the Infirmaress, use sign language to signal her to finish quickly and follow her to the church. Katherine obeyed, washing her hands in the bowl of cold water and drying them on the towel that hung nearby. Then she followed her aunt out of the convent hospital, through the cloister and joined the line of nuns entering the church.

Katherine barely noticed the cold spring wind that whipped her long white skirt around her legs and tugged at her black veil. With her arms tucked comfortably inside her long sleeves, she walked up the dark stone church steps lost in thought. Her thoughts were troubling ones. She had lived in the Marienthron nunnery for fourteen years, sent there by her father when she was ten years old. In fact, Katherine remembered very little of her home or family. Her mother had died when she was very young and her father had sent her to another convent to go to school at that time. The people she remembered best were the nuns who had been her teachers and had cared for her along with other children who lived there. Growing up in the convent, she had learned to love the nun's way of life that was devoted to prayer and praise of God. And most important Katherine had come to love God. At the age of sixteen, Katherine had taken her vows to become a nun because she thought it was the very best way to serve God. Now she wasn't so sure.

Someone cleared her throat loudly, a sound that echoed in the silent church, and Katherine jerked her head up. She was standing on the stone steps leading up to the choir stalls where all of the nuns had taken their places. The Abbess, standing in the centre, glared at her and Katherine dipped her head in apology and moved quickly to take the last place. Standing beside Sister Ave, Katherine opened her mouth to join in the psalm of praise led by the Abbess. All the troubling thoughts went away while she sang and prayed, worshipping God as fervently as she could. But when they left the church to go to the refectory for supper, the thoughts returned. Was she really serving God the right way?

After supper the nuns were allowed an hour of recreation, either in the warming room around a comfortable fire or walking in the garden. This was the one time in the day when the women were allowed to speak freely to one another. In spite of the cold spring air Katherine, Ave and Margarete met in the garden as usual. Walking on the pathways between the beds that would sprout herbs and vegetables when the weather warmed, the young women spoke in soft tones to each other.

'I have received a letter from my father,' Margarete told them. 'He has refused to receive me back home. He says I should be happy to be dedicated to God and he would be in trouble with the church if he lets me come home.'

Both Katherine and Ave sighed. It was no surprise. Both their families had refused them too.

'What are we going to do now?' Ave asked. 'I read part of Dr. Luther's essay against monastery vows again this afternoon in the library. He's very clear that there is nothing in the Bible about making vows to serve God in a convent or monastery. In fact he says that the rules of the convent violate the first commandment, because we are putting man-made rules above Christ. Oh, what do we do? Dr. Luther says our vows are not binding and we shouldn't stay here.'

'I know,' Katherine replied. 'But we can't just leave. It's not allowed. And besides, we need somewhere to go. It isn't safe or right for a woman to live by herself.'

They continued walking, very troubled in their thoughts. They and others in the convent had spent the last year reading Dr. Luther's writings and his German translation of the Bible during their times of private study and devotion. Then during the recreation hour, they would discuss what it all meant and how the church was changing. Dr. Luther said the Pope was just a man, not God's special anointed one on earth. He said that righteousness came by having faith in God alone and that no one could 'pay' God with their deeds or promises. And then he told monks and nuns they should leave their monasteries and nunneries and not follow the man-made rules. But following those rules was just what Katherine had been doing most of her life!

'If Dr. Luther thinks we should give up being nuns, maybe we should ask him how,' Katherine said aloud and then stopped walking when she realised Ave and Margarete had stopped too.

'You can't!' Ave said in a shocked tone.

'Why not?' Katherine demanded. 'He told us to leave, but not how. Shouldn't he have to help us since it was his idea in the first place?'

'But he didn't write those essays just to us. They were for all Germany to read. Why would such a great man bother with us?' Margarete protested.

'Because it's his duty,' Katherine replied with more certainty than she felt.

Just then the bell sounded to call them to Compline. Obeying the bell all three ceased their conversation and left the garden to go to the church.

As they entered the courtyard between the garden and the cloister, Katherine saw Mr. Koppe's large wagon pull in through the gate. She immediately had an idea. Leonhard Koppe was a merchant who visited the nunnery regularly, bringing in salted herring and other items that the convent couldn't provide for itself. As a follower of Luther, he had also brought in some of the pamphlets and a copy of the German Bible they all read now. Katherine wasn't sure the Abbess knew about these secret deliveries, and since no one had complained the nuns just shelved them in the library making them available to whoever wanted to read them. If Mr. Koppe could bring things into the convent, surely he could take things out. Things such as a letter to Dr. Luther asking for his help.

A month later Katherine was in the garden once more, reading Dr. Luther's reply to the nun's plea for help. Six other nuns were crowding around, all wanting a chance to read the letter too. Knowing they should all be walking instead of standing about in clusters, Katherine quickly passed the letter to someone else and followed her aunt, Sister Magdalene, down the pathway.

'Will you come too?' Katherine asked her. Her heart pounded with excitement as she thought of the proposed plan of escape.

'Yes,' Sister Magdalene replied. 'I have become convinced that Dr. Luther is right. I seem to have wasted so many years here,' she finished sadly.

'You didn't know the truth then, but now you do. Surely God hears our pleas for forgiveness,' Katherine tried to reassure her. 'It will be so hard to carry on as usual knowing we are leaving on Easter weekend.'

The week passed very slowly for Katherine. In some ways she was very sad to leave a place that had been her home and all the familiar routines of the convent. In other ways she could hardly contain her excitement. She was going to live in the outside world, hopefully marry and have children, something she had taken a vow never to do. She had thought her vow to remain unmarried was what God had wanted, but now she knew better. She could serve

God by being a good wife and mother.

The Saturday before Easter Katherine and eleven other nuns all followed the usual routines of the convent, except that instead of going to sleep after Compline, they each crept out of their small cells and met in the shadows of the cloister walkway. No one spoke as they waited for Mr. Koppe to signal that the way was clear.

His large wagon stood where it had been since the afternoon, to one side of the courtyard. He had arrived with a delivery and his helpers, but they had taken their time with the unloading. Some of the herring barrels still stood beside the wagon. He and the two young men had been given dinner in the kitchen by the convent servants and were just now emerging into the darkening evening.

Mr. Koppe, an older man with a rounded belly, spoke to his helpers in normal tones, instructing them to start loading the barrels. Then with hand signals, he motioned to the group of nuns to come forward one at a time.

Ave, the youngest, went first. Mr. Koppe pointed to where she was to sit in the large wagon as she climbed in. One of the young men lifted a large wooden barrel with ease and set it into the wagon. Katherine was next as she climbed past Ave. And so it went; first a nun and then a barrel was loaded

until all were squeezed in tightly, nuns and strongly smelling fish barrels. Some snuck inside the empty barrels, other squeezed inbetween them. Lastly, Mr. Koppe threw blankets over the top of them to hide them from view.

Katherine felt the wagon shift as the three men climbed aboard the wagon and heard Mr. Koppe call out to the porter.

'Open the gate, if you please. We are loaded and ready to go.'

Then the wagon lurched forward as the horses began to move. Katherine felt herself being pushed into Ave as the fish barrel beside her shifted. Straightening her back she pushed back at the barrel.

'Sorry,' she whispered, as her friend struggled to keep her balance.

'I think we'll all be badly bruised at the end of this journey,' Margarete muttered nearby.

Then they were quiet. No one in the town of Grimma, just outside the convent, must know there were people hiding in the wagon. Mr. Koppe and his helpers would be arrested and the nuns returned to the convent to be severely punished. Onward the wagon went, lurching over the rutted roads. The journey lasted all night and each weary hour was punctuated with hills and valleys. Going uphill meant they and the barrels all slid downward. Katherine and Ave clung together, trying to stay in place. Going downhill meant the opposite. Then Katherine and Ave had to put their backs against the barrels and push to keep them from crushing them against the front of the wagon. At one point they heard voices shouting and running feet. Ave gripped Katherine's arm in fear. Had they been discovered?

Once the sound of voices receded, Mr. Koppe pulled back the blankets letting in some welcome fresh air. The sky overhead was black and obscured in part by tree branches. They must be in a forest.

'Be at peace, ladies,' Mr. Koppe said. 'Those voices were peasants angry at their lord. They know nothing of your escape and showed no interest in us. We will move as quickly as the horses allow, but we must also be cautious. The duke of this state is an enemy of Dr. Luther so we must not bring attention to ourselves. Once we are close to the town of Torgau, all will be safe. So do your best to stay quiet and pray for our safety.'

Then he covered them up with the blankets once more and the wagon began to move. Katherine and Ave gripped hands and silently prayed for God's mercy and safekeeping.

Just as Katherine thought the journey would never end, the wagon stopped and the blankets were lifted from overhead. This time along with the sweet smelling air, sunlight tumbled in making them all close their eyes for a moment. Then they heard the bells of the town ringing out the joy of Easter Sunday.

'Christ has risen!' Sister Magdalene called out.

'He has risen indeed,' all the other nuns responded with the customary Easter greeting.

Katherine could have shouted for joy as she slowly stood up letting the blood return to her cramped legs. How fitting they should have arrived on the best day in the Christian calendar, the day to celebrate Jesus' resurrection from the grave. She too felt like she was starting a new life, one that would be dedicated to God in the way he commanded.

The two young men helped each of the twelve women down from the wagon in the town square. Their white habits were smudged and wrinkled, their black veils askew. They rubbed their arms and stretched their backs to get the kinks out of their cramped muscles. But in spite of all the stiffness, they each wore wide smiles on their faces. People began to gather, wondering how these somewhat dishevelled nuns smelling of fish had arrived in their town.

Mr. Koppe, also smiling, opening his arms wide and said, 'Welcome to Torgau, my ladies. We will provide a place for you to tidy up. Tomorrow I will take you on to Wittenberg where you will meet Dr. Luther himself.'

'Thank you, Mr. Koppe for your bravery in rescuing us,' Sister Magdalene replied. Then turning to the other nuns, 'Now we should go to church,'

'Yes,' Katherine agreed. 'We have much to thank God for.'

If you want to read more about Katherine von Bora you will find her in *Ten Girls who made a Difference* by Irene Howat

ISBN: 978-1-85792-776-4

Devotional Thought:

We have escaped like a bird from the snare of the fowlers; the snare is broken, and we have escaped! Our help is in the name of the LORD, who made heaven and earth. Psalm 124:7-8

These verses remind us of how God helps us in difficult situations. Sometimes you may feel as though you are like a bird that has been captured, but is set free at just the last moment when the snare holding it is broken. Katherine must have felt a little like that bird when she was escaping from the convent. If she and the other nuns had been caught, they would have been severely punished. But her help came from the Lord, the one who made and controls all things.

Katherine arrived safely in the town of Wittenberg where she met Martin Luther. He was concerned to find husbands and homes for all the escaped nuns, which he did over the next two years. He ended up marrying Katherine himself and they were very happy together. They had a family of six children. Katherine was well known for her manager skills. She ran a farm and a brewery, took care of her family and also cared for the students who came to live with them. As many as thirty students lived with them at one time, all eager to be taught by Dr. Martin Luther. Martin lovingly called Katherine 'My lord Katy.'

GERMANY

FACT FILE

The nation of Germany is often on the news and it is certainly in your history books. But in Martin Luther's time Germany as we know it today didn't even exist. It was originally a collection of tribes which then later became a group of states ruled by princes and an Emperor. In the 1800s the German Confederation was formed   a loose league of thirty-nine sovereign states. It wasn't until 1871 that the state known as Germany was unified and the German Empire was formed. After the two world wars Germany was again split in 1945 into two nations - West and East Germany. In 1990 after mass demonstrations in the Communist East both West and East Germany were reunited to form one nation again.

FIDELIA FISKE

Fidelia Fiske lived from 1816-1864. She was born in Shelburne, Massachusetts in the United States. Fidelia grew up in a Christian home and was converted when she was fifteen years old. Fidelia was a very bright student and she went on to study at the first university for women in the United States. When she graduated from Mount Holyoak Female Seminary she became a teacher there. Fidelia had suffered a terrible bout of typhoid when she was younger which left her with poor health. So when she suddenly announced after a year as a teacher that she felt called to be a missionary to Persia (now Iran), her friends and family told her she was foolish to go. After much prayer and discussion, Fidelia went anyway. In those days the only way to travel to another continent was by boat and then by horse or donkey. No one thought Fidelia would even survive the four month journey. But God protected her and she arrived in the large city of Orumiyeh to run a school for girls. Not a dangerous thing to do, you would think. But it turned out to be very dangerous indeed.

PERSECUTION IN PERSIA
SUMMER 1848

*A*man's deep voice shouted out across the busy throng of people. 'Don't listen to that Satan called Fidelia Fiske!'

Fidelia heard those words and came to a sudden stop. She and two of her older students were walking briskly through the stone streets of Orumiyeh in Northern Persia on their way back to the mission school. They stopped too and looked around anxiously to see who was speaking. Then they noticed the people were all walking in one direction, to the marketplace, a large open courtyard in the centre of the city. But no one was buying food or clothing today. As they cautiously followed the crowd of Persian people, Fidelia saw they were gathering around the Nestorian leader, Mar Shimon, a strong muscular man with a heavy black beard. He stood on the stone steps of a building speaking to the people.

Mar Shimon shouted. 'Take your daughters out of her school and have nothing to do with her teachings.'

Fidelia pulled the girls back into the shadows of a doorway. Her western style of dress with its wide hooped skirt made her easily seen in the midst of men and women dressed in their colourful Persian linen tops and flowing trousers. And she didn't want her students standing in the crowd without her protection. Fidelia's heart pounded as she listened to Mar Shimon continue to rail against the missionaries and their work. The crowd muttered and shifted restlessly, some calling out their agreement as the hot sun beat down on them.

Just then everyone's attention turned away from Mar Shimon to the sounds of Psalm 46 being sung by a group of new Persian Christians. Fidelia peered out of her hiding place to see a funeral procession as it rounded the corner. In the centre of the group of mourners was a man carrying a small coffin. Everyone in the mob moved aside to let the funeral procession pass, all the while looking uneasily at Mar Shimon as he stood with his arms crossed against his bright red robe. He glared in anger at them, but he said nothing until the people had passed through and disappeared around a corner. Everyone knew he had tried to stop that funeral of a baby girl because her father had become a Christian, but the Persian governor intervened and told Mar Shimon for the sake of peace to let the parents bury their child. Mar Shimon had obeyed, but he now had plans for revenge. So as soon as the mob turned back to him, he began to shout once more.

'We must stop these American devils from taking our children and teaching them! Close the schools in the villages and their churches too!'

Cries of agreement rose from the mob and the men began to leave, pouring out through the city gates. Fidelia and the girls flattened themselves against wall in the doorway, praying that none of the angry men would see them. Then, when it looked as if the way were clear, Fidelia and her companions ran as quickly as they could through the winding stone streets to the mission grounds.

Over fifteen years ago the Muslims of the city had kindly given the American missionaries land to build their mission house and schools. The Nestorian people had welcomed the missionaries too. But now their attitude was changing. The Nestorians were not pleased when Fidelia wanted to teach their girls. They thought that girls didn't need to go to school to get married and be mothers. But when one Nestorian

leader finally sent his daughter and niece, others followed.

Fidelia found that the girls were eager to learn to read and write and hear about God's Word. Many of the girls had been converted, and they returned to their villages to share the gospel with their families and friends. This made Nestorian leaders angry.

Arriving at the mission grounds, Fidelia called out, 'Shut the gate,' as she ran in the garden.

The other missionaries heard her calling and came out of the various buildings to see what the fuss was about. Fidelia could see her girls leaning out of the windows full of curiosity. As Mr. and Mrs. Perkins and Mr. and Mrs. Stevens began to question them, Fidelia stumbled out an account of the funeral and Mar Shimon's speech. 'We can't send the girls home at the end of the term,' Fidelia said. 'They will certainly be harmed, either by their unbelieving families or the mob. They would be much safer with us here where we can close the gate and keep those people out.'

'If we can keep them out,' Mrs. Steven shuddered.

'We will do all we can to protect ourselves,' Mr. Stevens assured his wife. 'The gate is strong and so are the stone walls. And God has graciously given us many converts among the local people. I'm sure they will help us.'

Later that week one of the Christian men arrived at the mission house with news that many of the village schools had been closed.

'They beat our teachers and tore up the books,' he reported as he gratefully drank some cold water. 'They closed our church too, but that didn't stop us worshipping,' he added with a small smile. 'We met on the rooftop of someone's house and sang psalms and listened to God's Word.'

Mr. Perkins nodded. 'I have heard similar reports from others. And I suspect it won't stop there. I'm sure it won't be long before Mar Shimon comes back to the city to deal with us. We must be much in prayer, putting on the whole armour of God for the fight ahead.'

Fidelia and her students listened closely to what Mr. Perkins had said and returned to their two-storey mud brick school across the fragrant herb garden to hold a prayer meeting of their own.

Several weeks passed and then the mob arrived. They could hear the noise in the streets. Rushing to the window, Fidelia saw the young Christian Persian carpenter who had made the coffin for the baby girl last month being dragged along and beaten.

'Away from the windows,' she ordered, and gathered the frightened girls around her. Taking time to hug each one, she said, 'Our time would be better spent praying for that man and for ourselves. We must be ready to face the same fate if God wills it.'

Fidelia began to pray, asking God for courage. As much as she loved God and his people she was still afraid for herself and her girls. What would happen if the mob ever broke through the gates into the mission grounds?

That night they all lay down on their sleeping mats in the school room listening to the noise and confusion in the city streets. Before turning down the lamps, Fidelia read Psalm 4 to them, repeating the last verse to remind them of God's care for them.

In peace I will both lie down and sleep; for you alone, O Lord, make me dwell in safety.

The next day as they assembled for their morning meal a messenger arrived for Sarah, one of the students. Sarah and Fidelia went to meet the man in the school room.

'Uncle!' Sarah said with surprise and greeted him with a kiss. 'What has happened?'

Fidelia stood to one side watching as the older man told Sarah her brother was very ill and might die soon. 'You must come home at once. He is asking for you,' her uncle urged. The man glanced over at Fidelia with an unfriendly look.

Sarah, too, looked to her teacher. 'Miss Fiske, I

must go to my brother. May I leave immediately?'

Fidelia hesitated. Something didn't seem quite right. Finally she said, 'Go and finish your morning meal first, then you may pack your things. And your uncle may join us too.'

The older man stiffened. 'No, I will wait for her by the gate.' And he left.

Sarah returned to the kitchen and her fellow students, while Fidelia sat down to think. What if Sarah's family were just trying to take her away from the school and then not allow her to return? As she wondered who to ask, she saw Mr. Stevens walk into the garden outside the school. He had just come back from a journey near Sarah's village. Maybe he would know. So she rushed out to the garden, calling his name.

Before Fidelia could ask Mr. Stevens her question, he asked her one. 'What is that man doing by the mission gate? Don't you know he is one of Mar Shimon's men?'

'So that explains it,' Fidelia replied. 'He is Sarah's uncle and wants her to come home because her brother is ill. I knew he wasn't to be trusted.'

Mr. Perkins shook his head. 'I saw Sarah's father several days ago. He said nothing about his son being ill. I wouldn't believe what Sarah's uncle tells you.'

Fidelia gathered up her long hooped skirt and headed for the mission gate where the man was waiting. 'Sarah will stay here. I know about your lies,' she announced to the startled man and stood with her arms folded in front of her.

'I will tell Mar Shimon about this and you'll be sorry!' he shouted and shook his fist at her.

Two days later again loud knocking was heard at the gates and when they were opened in fell a teacher from one of the village schools. He was bleeding and limping from a beating.

'Wait, don't close the gate,' he called out as they tried to lead him inside the mission house. 'My brother was following me, trying to outrun the mob. Please let him in.'

As he finished speaking another man ran through the open gate and collapsed on the ground. 'Close it, quick,' he gasped. Mr. Perkins slammed the gate shut and put the bar across it just as the shouts of the mob could be heard down the street. Then they helped both men into the house.

As Fidelia and Mrs. Perkins cleaned their wounds and bandaged them, the men told how the mob had assaulted them in their homes, chasing away their family and servants and then tried to destroy their houses. The teacher and his brother managed to escape and lead the mob away from the village. Then it became a foot race to the city and to the safety of the mission house.

As they finished their story one of the mission workers burst into the room. 'Come quick. The mob is trying to break down the gate. They are threatening to kill everyone.'

Mr. Perkins took charge, giving orders to the women to take the girls to the school while the men, both missionaries and the local men who also followed Jesus, to guard the gate and watch the walls. Fidelia, Mrs. Stevens and Mrs. Perkins herded their charges in the school room where everyone knelt down and began to pray. Fidelia prayed for their safety and that God would stop the mob from hurting anyone. Then she prayed that God would change the hearts of the Shah and his governors so they would send soldiers to stop the persecutions.

After several hours the mob grew tired of shouting at the missionaries and, unable to break down the strong wooden gate, they went off in search of others they could harass. Everyone in the mission grounds sighed with relief and again knelt in prayer, this time to thank God for his protection.

The city was unsettled for days afterwards. Fidelia could hear shouting and gun fire throughout the day and night coming from various parts of the city. It was difficult to sleep and always worrisome that the mob would come back. But later that month news arrived that heartened the entire mission.

Mr. Perkins called the entire group together in the garden. 'I have heard that the Shah died a short time ago. God has answered our prayers. His son will be the new shah and he is much more tolerant toward our work here. People like Mar Shimon will be told to stop their violence.'

Everyone knelt down on the grassy areas and stone pathways and thanked God for his deliverance.

It was sometime before the city became quiet and ordered again. But later that month Fidelia wrote a letter to her mother about what had happened. She finished with

'But, thanks to our heavenly Father, those exciting days are past, and we hope that some degree of order may soon be restored to poor Persia. The young king has been crowned, and all is quiet at the capital. After the death of the king, Mar Shimon retired into Turkey, but was soon driven back for a season by fear of the Kurds. He did not, however, dare any longer to oppose the mission or the native Christians.'

Devotional Thought:

If the world hates you, know that it has hated me before it hated you. If you were of the world, the world would love you as its own; but because you are not of the world, but I chose you out of the world, therefore the world hates you. Remember the word that I said to you: "A servant is not greater than his master." If they persecuted me, they will also persecute you. If they kept my word, they will also keep yours. John 15:18-20.

Jesus said those words to his disciples just before he was arrested by the Roman soldiers. He was warning them that they would be treated just as he was being treated...arrested, beaten, laughed and spat at and even killed. Not a very encouraging thing to say to his followers, was it? But it was a good warning, because just as people didn't want to hear the truth from the Son of God himself, people still don't want to hear Christians speak about God's truth. Fidelia learned that in Persia. She could have been a teacher and stayed in America, where she would have been safe. Instead she obeyed God's call to go far away to teach girls not only how to read and write, but about God's love. It was the right thing to do, but also a hard thing. God gave Fidelia the courage she needed and kept her safe. Fidelia was able to stay in Persia for another ten years teaching Persian girls. Then her health declined and she had to return home. She was sad to leave because even though there had been much danger and persecution, she loved the Persian people.

If you want to read something else about Fidelia Fiske you will come across her in the History Lives book: *Hearts and Hands, Chronicles of the Awakening Church* by Mindy and Brandon Withrow.

ISBN: 978-1-84550-288-1

PERSIA

FACT FILE

What we now refer to as the nation of Iran was formerly known as Persia until 1935. On 21 March 1935 Iran was officially accepted as the new name of the country. It is a country situated in Central Eurasia and located on the northeastern shore of the Persian Gulf and the southern shore of the Caspian Sea. In the Bible in the story of Daniel reference is made to 'The Medes and the Persians.' After Daniel was captured in his homeland he was taken to Babylon as a slave. Babylon was a city that was captured by the Persians in 539 BC when it fell to Cyrus the Great, King of Persia.

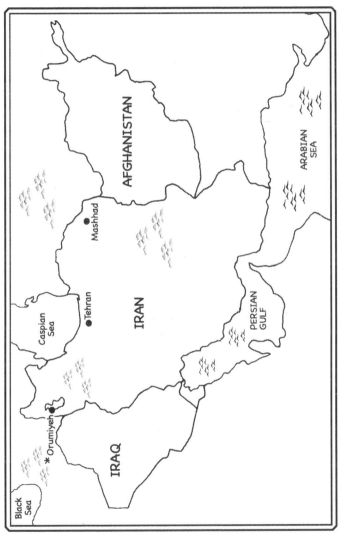

* Orumiyeh is the old name for Urmia.

AMY CARMICHAEL

my Carmichael lived from 1867-1951. She was born in Millisle, Northern Ireland and was the oldest of seven children. Amy grew up in a Christian home and was converted when she was eighteen. After she heard the missionary, Hudson Taylor, speak at a Keswick Convention she felt called to be a missionary too. She went to Japan first and then, 'as if by accident' she ended up in India. But there are no accidents with God. Amy had to learn quickly about the caste system there. Everyone was born into a caste, which was controlled by the Hindu religion. Each caste had certain things that they could or could not do, certain occupations, and only certain people they could talk to or marry. No one mixed with someone from another caste. So imagine how bad it was for someone who would not follow the caste system rules....someone who decided to follow Jesus instead of the Hindu gods. Amy found out.

Amy is best known for the orphanage that she opened in Dohnavur which is situated in Tamil Nadu, thirty miles from the southern tip of India.

A FURIOUS FAMILY

SEPTEMBER-OCTOBER 1898

Amy Carmichael sighed with the heat as she bounced about in the bandy cart, a small covered wagon pulled by a plodding ox. The large white beast seemed to object to the heat too because she bellowed every so often and the driver had to shout at her in Tamil to urge her to keep moving. Amy shifted a little which caused the three other women, her Indian co-workers, in the cart to move too. They were part of what Amy called the 'Starry Cluster,' Indian women who had chosen to follow Jesus. Together they travelled to small villages in southern India to share the gospel with others.

As the cart came to a halt, the women untangled their saris and slid out. Amy, dressed in a white Indian sari too so as not to stand out too much as an Irish woman, stretched and looked at the village spread out below in a small green valley.

'We need to pray,' she announced, and all the women knelt by the cart. This was their usual custom, asking God to lead them to people who needed to hear the gospel.

Armed with prayer and purpose the women entered the village. Amy directed Pearl and Blessing to go down one street, while she and Ponnammal started down the other.

Part way down the street they came to a large Nim tree, offering a welcome pool of shade to sit in. 'This will do nicely,' Amy said as she sat down. Ponnammal followed her example and then opened up a canvas bag she had been carrying.

It didn't take long before a young woman carrying a basket stopped to greet them and enjoy a moment in the shade. Amy invited her sit with them. 'We have a book we would like to show you,' she said.

As the woman settled herself, Ponnammal drew out of her bag the Wordless Book. Just as Amy was about to explain the colourful pages, several other women began to gather around. Amy welcomed them with a smile and invited them to sit down too.

'I have some Good News to share with you,' Amy said. The children crowded in close and had to be shooed back to allow an elderly lady to see. Using the colours on each page, Amy told them the story of how we are all black because of sin in our hearts, and how Jesus' blood can wash away that sin, making us clean as white linen and give us eternal life in a golden heaven. Everyone listened politely and Amy felt encouraged to ask if any of them would like to become Christians. Shaking her head hard, the oldest woman muttered about never breaking caste and shook her bony finger at the children. They stepped back respectfully and refused to look at the Wordless Book again. Then a man's voice was heard, calling from down the street. The young woman rose hastily and gathered up her basket. The others began to drift away.

Amy and Ponnammal exchanged discouraged glances and thanked the women for listening to them. It always seemed to happen this way. People listened politely as she explained the gospel, some even asked questions, but none wanted to break away from their families or their Hindu religion. Their families threatened to kill them if they did. Sometimes husbands and fathers yelled at Amy, telling her to leave their wives and daughters alone.

When Amy met up with the others at the bandy cart at the end of the morning, they too reported the same thing. No one had responded to the good news that morning.

'All the more reason to keep praying and keep trying,' Amy thought. 'We are here to fight against the Kingdom of Darkness. Please, O God, give us strength to carry on.' And so Amy kept praying that soon someone would have the courage to follow Jesus. The next month God answered her prayer.

'Amma, come quick,' Ponnammal rushed into Amy's bedroom where she had just risen from prayer.

Amy straightened up the folds of her white sari and asked calmly. 'What is it, Ponnammal?'

Taking Amy by the arm, the young woman all but dragged Amy out of the room, speaking rapidly. 'Remember Preetha, the girl you spoke with yesterday about Jesus? She is here! She wants to break her caste and follow Jesus. But she is very afraid.'

Amy gave a silent prayer of thanksgiving to God and quickened her pace to follow the excited Indian woman into the next room. A teenaged Indian girl, dressed in a sky blue sari, stood there looking very worried. Amy suppressed the urge to rush over and hug Preetha. Amy knew Indian people didn't think it was right to be touched by people who were not part of their caste. So Amy led Preetha to some chairs where they sat together.

'Tell me,' Amy said softly.

Preetha's brown eyes were full of tears, but her

voice was strong. 'I must follow Jesus,' she replied. 'When you told me how he died for me, how Jesus suffered to save me from the darkness in my soul, I couldn't sleep. I knew I must follow him. So I have come and I will stay here with you. I need to know more about God.'

Amy could hardly contain her joy. Weary week after weary week, Amy had prayed and shared the good news and now at last someone had responded.

At that moment heavy footsteps were heard on the veranda outside. Preetha leapt up in fear. Amy too stood up, but recognizing the tread, calmed the frightened girl. 'It's only the Walkers, my missionary friends, returning home. We will need their help when your family comes.' Preetha gave a gasp at the thought of her family. 'Never mind,' Amy continued. 'We will stand with you and God will protect us all.'

That evening at dinner, Amy helped Preetha tell Thomas and Mary Walker how Preetha had left her home and family to become a Christian. Thomas began to talk about what they could do to protect Preetha.

'The family will blame us as well as her. They may try to harm us.'

'Then we will stand firm,' Amy declared, ready to fight for God. 'Doesn't the Bible say we must forsake all to follow Jesus? Preetha is doing just that and we mustn't back down just because there's danger.'

The Walkers nodded in agreement and then together they prayed for strength and protection.

Sometime in the night, Amy began to hear voices outside the house. It started softly, but as more people gathered, the noise grew. Preetha, sleeping in the same room, woke up with a frightened start. 'Are they here?' she asked in a whisper.

'Yes,' Amy replied. 'Are you ready to meet them?'

Preetha nodded. Amy knew the next few days were going to be very difficult and dangerous. So as they wound their saris around themselves and put on their sandals, Amy never stopped praying. Then, together with the Walkers, they went out and stood on the veranda.

The hot night was lit by torches carried by some of the men from Preetha's caste. A large group of both men and women stood around, and some of the women began to cry loudly when Preetha appeared. Preetha's mother rushed up to the steps and began to plead with her daughter to come back to her family. 'We are your people!' she cried out. 'Come back to us.' And she began to beat her chest and wail. Others in the group also called out, 'Come back!' and the noise grew with their chanting.

Mr. Walker, afraid a riot would break out, urged Amy to take Preetha back inside.

'I want my daughter back,' a tall man pushed forward to stand by his wife who was still wailing. 'See what she does to her mother with her foolish behaviour? If she must be a Christian then she can be one in our house. We will let her go to church.'

Amy knew the man wasn't telling the truth and so did Preetha. They had heard the stories about what happened to women who tried to be Christians in a Hindu caste. Their families usually killed them, either starving them or giving them poison in their food. It was considered a terrible thing for a Hindu person to become a Christian.

Inside the house once more, Amy watched from the windows as Preetha's family set up camp in the front yard. They were not giving up. They wanted their daughter back. All through the night and the next day, they pleaded through the windows, calling for Preetha to come home. Her mother even lay on the veranda thumping her head on the wood hoping Preetha would feel guilty and come out. But inside, Amy and Ponnammal were praying with Preetha and reading the Bible with her, teaching her more about God.

Finally as the night approached, Amy and the Walkers decided to take some action.

'Do you feel strong enough to face your family?' Amy asked Preetha. 'We will stand with you, but you must be the one to say if you are staying or going back.'

'I am ready,' she replied.

Once more the Walkers, Amy and Preetha came out into the hot night air and faced Preetha's family. Preetha was shaking with fear.

Mr. Walker called out. 'We have had enough of this. Preetha is free to go. We are not holding her against her will.' Then he turned to the girl. 'Do you choose to go with your family?'

Preetha stood tall and called out in a loud voice, 'NO!'

An angry roar erupted from her family. Voices called out threats to harm Preetha. Others said they would send lawyers or police to get her. Some wailed and cried, still pleading with her to come home. Amy rushed Preetha back into the house, away from the threatening crowd of her relatives.

No one slept that night. The noise of Preetha's family carried on as they shouted threats. At one point Amy looked out the window and saw someone had set fire to the mission school, but there was nothing they could do about it. It was not safe to leave the house.

For days Preetha's family held them hostage but Preetha grew more certain she must follow Jesus and told her family so. They would not listen. Each day, Amy, Ponnammal and the Walkers spent their time in prayer and studying God's Word.

At last it was decided that Preetha must get away. Amy offered to take her to another mission house in Palamcottah.

'We can sneak out tonight, if you and Mrs. Walker will keep them busy talking,' Amy said. 'We can creep through the forest to where our bandy cart is lodged and ask our driver to take us.'

Mr. Walker was hesitant to send them both into danger. But if he took Preetha himself, then he would leave his wife unprotected. And all four of them could not all go without Preetha's family noticing right away.

So it was decided. They waited until full dark had fallen. Amy and Preetha, dressed in dark coloured saris waited by the back door for the signal from Mrs. Walker when to leave. Then Mr. Walker opened the front door and stepped out onto the wide veranda. While he listened to yet more calls for Preetha to come home and the threats to himself, Amy and Preetha quietly opened the back door. Slowly they edged their way to the trees, keeping to the shadows so that no one looking their way would see them moving. After gaining the protection of the forest, they quickened their pace, using the light of the moon to see, until they arrived at the shed where a small covered wagon stood. They roused the driver, who slept inside, and he went to get the ox that pulled the cart. Amy hoped they were far enough away that no one heard the ox's complaints.

Their journey to the next mission house was bumpy but uneventful. Once there, Preetha began to lose her worried fearful look. She hungrily studied the Bible wanting to know as much as she could about Jesus and his love. A month later, Preetha asked to be baptised, declaring to those around her that she was now a Christian. As was the custom she was given a new name. Amy selected one that translated into English as Jewel of Victory. Indeed God had given them a victory against the Kingdom of Darkness.

Devotional Thought:

If anyone comes to me and does not hate his own father and mother and wife and children and brothers and sisters, yes, and even his own life, he cannot be my disciple. Whoever does not bear his own cross and come after me cannot be my disciple. Luke 14: 26–27.

Jesus said these words to his disciples to make them understand how important their decision to follow him was. He didn't want his disciples to stop loving others. What he was saying is that God must come first even before the people we love. And if the people we love try to stop us from following Jesus then we must choose God. We must even give up our own desires to do what God tells us to do.

Preetha had to learn that when she became a Christian she had to turn away from the false religion of Hinduism. She even had to leave her family, risking her life in order to follow Jesus. Preetha's family could have harmed her or even killed her because of her new found faith in the Lord Jesus Christ. Amy helped Preetha by standing with her, taking the same risks and teaching her about God.

Amy went on to work in India for the rest of her life. A couple of years after this story, Amy began rescuing babies no one wanted and young children sold to the Hindu temples. She started an orphanage to care for them and they all called her Amma, the Tamil name for mother.

If you want to find out more about Amy Carmichael you can read about her life in

Amy Carmichael: Rescuer by Night by Kay Walsh

ISBN: 978-185792-946-1

INDIA

FACT FILE

For most of Amy Carmichael's life the nation of India was part of the British Empire. However, just before her death in 1951 great changes took place.

Before British rule India had been governed by different powers such as the Gupta Dynasty and the Delhi Sultanate and later the Mughal Empire. By 1856 most of India was under the control of the British East India company. After India's First War of Independence the British Crown took control of the country. In the 20th century however a new struggle for independence arose led by people like Mahatma Gandhi. On 15th August 1947 India gained independence from British rule. At the same time the nation of Pakistan was also formed.

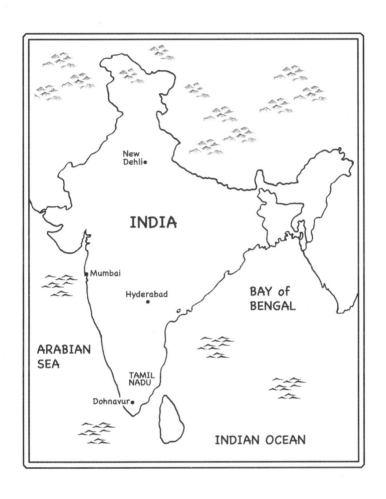

New
Dehli●

INDIA

● Mumbai

Hyderabad
●

BAY of
BENGAL

ARABIAN
SEA

TAMIL
NADU

Dohnavur●

INDIAN OCEAN

LILLIAN DICKSON

L illian LeVesconte Dickson lived from 1901–83. She was born in Prior Lake, Minnesota, in the United States into a Christian home.

When she went to college, two important things happened: God called her to be a missionary and she met her future husband, James Dickson. They were married one day after James graduated from seminary in 1927. Then they were ordained by the Canadian

Presbyterian Mission Board and left for Formosa (now Taiwan), an island off the coast of China. For the first twelve years, while James taught in the seminary in Taipei, Lillian spent her time raising their two young children, ministering to local women and children, and hosting many seminary and church functions. These were all necessary things to do, but there were times when Lillian must have wondered if she could have stayed in America and done the same thing. Then came the Second World War and the Japanese forced all the missionaries to leave the island. When they returned five years later, life changed for Lillian. Her children were away at school and her husband went back to teach at the seminary. But Lillian began to travel about the island visiting remote tribes in the mountains. Not an easy thing to do.

MOUNTAIN CLIMBER

AUGUST 1947

The rain fell gently down around Lillian, Eugenia and Hui-ben as they left the coastal city of Hualien in Formosa. Rain was nothing new in the tropical mountainous island, so Lillian thought nothing of it. She and Eugenia were missionaries along with their husbands. They had left their husbands teaching at the seminary in Taipei while they accompanied the Formosan Chinese pastor to visit some of the mountain tribes. Lillian had brought along flannelgraph stories to teach the children and Eugenia, a nurse, had brought some medical supplies.

They boarded the train knowing that this was the easiest part of the trip and they enjoyed the run from the ocean shore to the foot of the steep mountains where the town of Giok-li stood. As they disembarked from the train Lillian knew they were in for more than just a little rain.

'The wind is picking up,' she commented, her simple cotton dress flattened against her as she picked up her bag from the crowded platform. 'And smell the air.'

Hui-ben nodded. 'A typhoon is coming. We had better get to the inn quickly.'

All three followed the people of the town as they too scurried to their homes, gathering up children and calling out orders to close all the shutters and doors as tight as possible. The rain began in earnest and the trio arrived on the wooden porch of the inn soaked to the skin.

'Come in, come in,' the owner shouted above the wind. He practically pulled them inside and then struggled to get the door closed and bolted.

Within the hour the town was caught in the middle of the storm's fury. Lillian and Eugenia lay on the rough mats in their small room praying for safety and listening as winds roared around the building pulling at the shutters and shaking the walls. Eventually they fell into a restless sleep.

The next morning when Lillian opened up the shutters to look out of the window she wondered if the inn had sailed out into the sea. They were completely surrounded by water.

'Eugenia, come and see,' Lillian woke up her friend. Both women leaned out the window to see what was left of the town. Some houses had lost roofs or porches and most were flooded with fast flowing water. Looking up the mountainside, they could see all the terraced rice fields had turned into waterfalls. A pretty sight, but it meant the crops were ruined.

'At least the inn is dry,' Eugenia said as she quickly dressed. 'Let's go make sure Hui-ben is alright.'

Meeting up with the Chinese pastor a short time later, Lillian said cheerfully, 'I'm glad to see you are well and there is no harm done to the inn.'

'Oh, but it's going to be worse,' the owner moaned as he met them in the reception room. 'The dam part way up the mountain is old and they are saying it was damaged by the typhoon. If it breaks, the whole town will be washed away.'

'We had better leave now,' Hui-ben said.

'You can't. No one can,' the innkeeper replied. 'All the roads are flooded. You will never make it into the mountains. Everyone is looking to find pieces of wood and rope. They plan to tie themselves to the wood if the dam breaks and hope that they will be carried away safely rather than drowning.'

All three looked at each other, wondering where they would find large pieces of wood to act like boats. Then Lillian said, 'I guess we'd better pray that the dam holds, but either way we can only wait. Either the waters will go down or the dam will break. But if we survive I don't want to go back to Taipei. We have come this far and I think we should go up into the mountains as soon as possible.'

They were all determined to keep going if and when they could. This trip was partly to find out which mountain churches had survived the Second World War. Lillian Dickson and her husband, James, had come as young missionaries to Formosa in 1927, but they and all the other western missionaries had to leave in 1941. The Japanese leaders of Formosa were at war with the United States. They began burning Bibles and churches and telling all the Formosan Christians to stop believing in Jesus or they would be killed. Now that the war was over the Dicksons and others had returned to the mountainous island and they wanted to check on the remote villages, hoping that some of the Christians had survived.

Marooned in the inn, Lillian, Eugenia and Hui-ben had lots of time to fill. Fortunately they had brought their own food with them for the trip up the mountain. Now they were able to enjoy it since the inn was quickly running out of food because they had to feed all the staff and other guests. Lillian also decided the enforced rest was a good time to translate another of the Child Evangelism books into Formosan. So she and the Chinese pastor spent many hours discussing just the right words in the Formosan language to use and writing it all down. Before they realised it, a week had passed.

The flood waters had started to go down, but they revealed much damage. Roads, bridges and railroad tracks had all been washed out. Almost every house needed some repairs.

'You'll not be able to travel for at least a month,' the innkeeper predicted. But he didn't know the mountain men of Formosa very well.

The next day several men came down from the town of Mikasa, higher up in the mountains. Muddy but cheerful, they said, 'Mrs. Dickson, you can come up now. We have repaired the roads and pathways and they're passable. There are many people waiting to see you.'

'Wonderful,' Lillian replied. 'We'll pack up our things and leave today.'

After settling the bill with the innkeeper, the two middle-aged women and the young Chinese pastor followed their guides up the slippery mountain path above the town. But Lillian soon discovered that what mountain men considered passable was not what she had in mind.

After an hour's trek through the mountain forests, they came to a deep gorge with a rushing river down below. Ahead of them was what had once been a railroad bridge. The under part that supported the tracks had been washed away in the typhoon and all that was left was the track swaying dangerously across the gorge. Lillian came to a halt, unable to believe the Formosan mountain guide was telling her to take his hand as he stepped out onto the long bridge. The railroad ties groaned under the man's weight, but held in place.

'Heavenly Father,' Lillian prayed silently as she too stepped out onto the swaying bridge. 'I can't do this. You have to help me. Only for you would I even try this.'

God answered Lillian's prayer, guiding her feet to put them on the railroad ties that would hold her weight, avoiding those that would give way. She kept her eyes on her guide who seemed not at all worried they could fall through to the dangerous waters at any moment. Once on the other side, Lillian fell down to her knees too shaky to stand upright. She rested there while the others made their way across and they all stood safely on firm ground. Hui-ben offered a heartfelt prayer of thanks to God for all of them.

But that was only the first of several dangerous bridges they had to navigate. The last one was a huge

iron bridge that had been washed out of it moorings and lay on its side, sticking up out of the deep river.

'How will we get over this one?' Lillian asked.

Rather than explain, one of guides swung himself up, climbing the iron structure until he reached the top. Then he carefully balanced along an iron railing and walked to the other side. From there he smiled and motioned to them to follow him.

Lillian and Eugenia exchanged disbelieving looks. They were both in their forties and they were expected to climb this giant jungle-gym as if they were school children!

'These are the things they forget to tell you about missionary work,' Lillian remarked. Then she pointed to the group of mountain people starting to gather across the river to watch. 'They are either praying for us or laying wagers as to whether or not we will get across alive,' she whispered to Eugenia. Eugenia just shook her head.

So they prepared to follow. The men strapped the medical and teaching supplies to their backs. They all took off their shoes, thinking they would be less likely to slip in bare feet, and began the climb. 'I'm climbing for you, Lord,' Lillian prayed, 'so that I can share your gospel with these people. Please guide my steps.'

Once more God answered Lillian's prayer. She and the others pulled themselves up at the top and balanced precariously on the narrow rail. Edging carefully along one at a time they made it across without mishap.

After another short trudge up a mountain path following the village people, they arrived at a small church sitting in the clearing. Surrounded by tall cedar and cypress trees, the air was full of lovely scents. But all Lillian could think about was a place to lie down. The day had been full of more exercise and excitement than she had had in a long time.

To her delight the people had built a bedroom right next to the church for them to stay in. How she longed to go in there and take a nap. And a bath. She was covered in mud and perspiration. But the people were so happy to see them they begged the pastor to please lead a worship service right away.

How could I be so selfish? Lillian thought. They have not had a minister to preach to them for years. Bed can wait.

So they gathered in the small wooden church, where Lillian led the singing and Hui-ben preached. It was thrilling to see these people hungry to hear God's Word.

Afterwards, Hui-ben took Lillian and Eugenia aside.

'I have arranged for you both to have a bath,' he said. 'Come and see what they are preparing for you.'

As both women followed him around to the back of one of the small houses, Eugenia whispered to Lillian, 'How can we have a bath? The Formosan people don't have bathtubs.'

Hui-ben came to a stop at the pig pen, a three sided wooden stall that stood shoulder high. A large black and white pig was being herded out of the stall as they approached. As the women watched, two men laid down clean boards over the muddy ground and several others brought a huge iron kettle full of hot water and some small pails. Full of pride they motioned the two women to go in, handed them a new bar of soap and promised not to walk by the open side of the stall while they washed.

Lillian laughed with delight. 'Oh, Eugenia, aren't we fortunate? We're having a bath in a pig pen and we think we are privileged!'

They spent two days in the village, encouraging the Christians and sharing the gospel with unbelievers. Eugenia set up a small clinic for the sick. She cleaned out wounds and wrapped them and gave out quinine for those with malaria.

Before they left to go on to the next village, Eugenia offered to teach them some things about health and nutrition. The chief thanked her politely for the offer, and said. 'We would rather hear about God. We believe that if we are right with God, all other things will follow.' So once more the village gathered together to worship God in their wooden church.

When they left for the next hike across the mountains, Lillian fervently hoped there would be no more dangerous bridges to cross. It was a hard trek with pathways that seemed to go straight up and then straight down. They waded through smaller rushing streams with the occasional spill into the water. Lillian found that rather refreshing in the heat of the day. And so they went from village to village tucked away in the mountains amazed at how strong the native churches were after suffering persecution from the Japanese. Lillian had come to encourage them, thinking they were small and weak. Instead she came away full of the joy that the church had grown strong and spread among even the Tyal people, known for their fierce head hunting. In fact, the Christians in the Tyal village they visited were busy evangelizing the Bunan tribe close by.

When Lillian, Eugenia and Hui-ben arrived in the village called Reposan, the Christians asked them to speak to the Bunan village first. The Bunan chief greeted the pastor politely and agreed that his people should attend the church in the next village. So he lined them up and marched his people over to the Reposan church. But so many arrived there wasn't enough room in the church for both tribes. So the Tyal Christians gave up their seats in the church and stood outside so their neighbours could hear the pastor preach to them.

Lillian thanked God for the wonderful unselfish spirit of the mountain Christians. She also thanked God for giving her the strength to cross all those bridges, keeping her safe and allowing her to see the strong churches he had established in this remote part of the world.

Devotional Thought:

*If it had not been the LORD who was on our side—
let Israel now say—.... then the flood would have
swept us away, the torrent would have gone over
us; then over us would have gone the raging waters.
Psalm 124:1,4-5.*

In these verses the Psalmist is grateful to God for looking after him, especially during a time of flood. He may well have meant more than just a flood of water. Meaning instead any time that is very difficult or dangerous. But Lillian would have read those words in her Bible and remembered climbing through the mountains and crossing those wobbly bridges. God, who was on her side, took her safely across each time. Lillian needed great courage to face those difficulties and God gave that to her too.

Lillian spent the rest of her life in Formosa. She began writing long letters to the churches in North America telling them about the Formosan people and their needs. She set up orphanages and schools for the mountain tribes. She had hospitals and special places for leper patients built. She loved the mountain tribes' people and adopted Bi-lian, also known as Dolly, as her second daughter. She was such a tireless traveller, writer and worker that the mountain people gave her the nickname 'Typhoon Lil.'

TAIWAN
FACT FILE:

Lillian worked on the island that is known today as Taiwan. It is situated off the coast of mainline China. When she began work there it was called Formosa. Taipei City is the main city in Taiwan. This area of the world has seen many changes politically over the years. Japan and China have fought over the island of Taiwan for two centuries. At some points Taiwan was considered part of Japan and then after World War II it became part of China. Even today people disagree about who owns this area of the world. Those on mainland China and those on the island of Taiwan disagree very strongly.

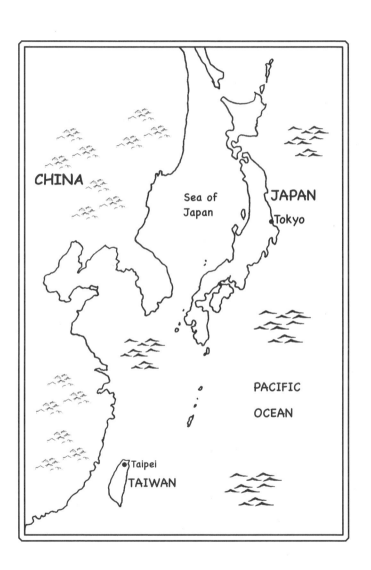

BIBLE CHARACTERS

You have now read four stories about women who lived in history. Even though they lived in different countries and at different times, they all loved God and took a risk to serve him. As they studied their Bibles, those women would have read many stories about Biblical women who also loved God and faced risks. The next two chapters are about a prophetess and a princess and how they chose to obey God, even when it was difficult and dangerous. They are good examples for us too.

DEBORAH,
THE ARMY CAPTAIN

Judges 4-5

Sometimes God calls people to do something they have never done before. And that can be a bit scary. God asked a woman named Deborah to do something no other woman had done in her country.

Deborah lived in Israel during the time after Joshua had led the Israelites into the Promised Land and before Saul became Israel's first king. Since there was no king to rule the country, God appointed judges. Judges were like prophets. God spoke to them, giving them directions to give to the people. The judges also did what judges do today, help people sort out problems between them and make wise decisions.

God had appointed Deborah to be a judge, a most unusual thing for a woman to do. But God cares about a person's heart and he knew that Deborah loved him and wanted to obey him in everything she did. So God spoke to Deborah and gave her the gift of wisdom, so that she could be a good judge for the people. The Bible tells us: 'Now Deborah, a prophetess, the wife of Lappidoth, was judging Israel at that time. She used to sit under the palm of Deborah between Ramah and Bethel in the hill country of Ephraim, and the people of Israel came up to her for judgment.' Judges 4:4-5.

During Deborah's time Israel had been invaded by Jabin, the king of Canaan. God allowed this to happen as a punishment.

> And the people of Israel again did what was evil in the sight of the LORD after Ehud died. And the LORD sold them into the hand of Jabin king of Canaan, who reigned in Hazor. Judges 4:1-2a.

Jabin was a cruel king and he made life miserable for the Israelites for over twenty years. They couldn't travel from village to village safely and they couldn't grow crops without the soldiers taking them. They grew hungry and more fearful with each year.

King Jabin had an army commander called Sisera who was the brilliant leader of a very large army that included nine hundred iron chariots. These were particularly terrifying to the Israelites because it was almost impossible for them to defeat them. So the people of Israel cried out to God to help them.

God heard their pleas for help and told Deborah to call a man named Barak, an Israelite who lived in the northern part of the country. Barak had been secretly gathering together an army of Israelite men and training them to fight against the strong army of Sisera, but he had not yet engaged the enemy in battle. He must have wondered as he travelled down through the hill country with his advisors what Judge Deborah would say to him.

When Barak arrived, he bowed respectfully to Deborah and waited to hear what God wanted him to do. Deborah had been given a rebuke from God for Barak and she must have wondered how Barak would feel when he heard God's words.

God said, "Has not the LORD, the God of Israel, commanded you, 'Go, gather your men at Mount Tabor, taking 10,000 from the people of Naphtali and the people of Zebulun. And I will draw out Sisera, the general of Jabin's army, to meet you by the river

Kishon with his chariots and his troops, and I will give him into your hand?"' Judges 4:6b-7.

Deborah reminded Barak that he had already been given instructions by God and he had been slow to obey. So she told him that he had to do as God had commanded him.

Barak's answer must have surprised Deborah. He didn't disagree with her.

He said instead: 'If you will go with me, I will go, but if you will not go with me, I will not go.' Judges 4:8.

Barak, the commander of a secret army, was asking a woman to help him lead them into battle. Was he being a coward, afraid of Sisera and his great army? Did he think Deborah would make a better leader than himself?

Barak knew Deborah was God's chosen prophet, and Barak thought that it could only help him and his army to have God's prophet with them. Deborah must have realised that too because she agreed even though she must have wondered how she could ever lead an army. She had no training with weapons or soldiers. But she did have God's promise that he would give them victory. It took great courage for her to say yes.

Deborah did give Barak a warning. Barak would not receive any glory from this battle. When people remembered this battle later, they would remember that a woman was the one who brought victory.

The fifty mile journey back through the hill country to Mount Tabor must have been difficult for Deborah. She was not used to climbing hills or fording rivers. But she insisted they press on as quickly as possible. It was important that God's command to defeat Sisera's army be obeyed.

Imagine how encouraging it would have been for all those Israelite men, secretly training in the mountains, to meet Deborah, God's appointed Judge. They must have worried about the battle to come. Would they be ready? Would they be brave even in the face of those menacing iron chariots racing down on them? After all, the Israelites only had swords and spears and no horses to ride. But here was God's prophetess reminding them of God's promise that he would defeat Sisera's army. It seemed impossible, but Deborah reminded them that nothing was impossible for God.

Soon Sisera heard about the Israelite army and called out his soldiers and chariots to start a march to the Kishon Valley at the foot of Mount Tabor. He must have thought he could easily defeat these poorly armed villagers, even if there were 10,000 of them. His men were well trained and his weapons much superior. He was full of confidence.

The day of the battle arrived. The Israelite army

stood ready at the top of Mount Tabor. Spread out below them in the valley next to the Kishon River stood Sisera and his huge army. Deborah, of course, would not fight, but as their commander in chief, she roused the Israelites with a speech.

Many would have been nervous, so Deborah gave them courage by praising their captains and reminding them that they were God's chosen people. God had promised them the victory if they would fight. Then the Israelite army, led by Barak, charged down the mountainside.

It must have seemed a very uneven match to Sisera. It was a battle between his strong army and a bunch of poor villagers. However, he didn't reckon with God's great power.

As the fight began, the weather began to change. From where Deborah stood on the mountain top, she could see black clouds begin to roll across the sky, pushed along by strong winds. Quickly the day darkened until it felt like twilight and spears of lightening began to pierce the thick clouds. As the thunderclaps resounded the clouds began to let loose a torrent of rain.

Below in the valley the Kishon River began to rise. Slowly at first, then lapping at the shore, and finally overflowing its banks, the water snaked its way across the flat plain of the valley between the

wheels of the mighty chariots and the horses' hooves. Puddles here and there joined with the advancing river and began to deepen, softening the earth and causing the heavy chariots to begin slowly sinking into the mud. At first no one really noticed what was happening. Then Deborah saw the horses begin to struggle to find their footing, causing their chariots to shift and slide. Sisera's soldiers began to cry out as they were dumped out of their chariots and into the mud. Barak and his army saw their chance and pressed the attack.

The Bible tells us: 'And the LORD routed Sisera and all his chariots and all his army before Barak by the edge of the sword. And Sisera got down from his chariot and fled away on foot.' Judges 4:15.

God had kept his promise and Sisera's army was completely defeated. But Sisera himself ran away. Barak saw the enemy commander flee and he followed him. The race was difficult in the rain and mud and Barak lost Sisera at one point. But he kept on searching for the commander, knowing if he let him get back to King Jabin Sisera would raise another army against Israel. After a long time of searching Barak found Commander Sisera....dead.

Remember how Deborah had told Barak that God would give the victory to a woman? What Deborah didn't say was who that woman would be. Not far away, near the town of Kedesh, lived a man called Heber and his wife, Jael. Heber had made a truce with King Jabin to protect his family and wealth, so Sisera considered him a friend. As Sisera ran from Barak he arrived at the tents of Heber, out of breath and needing a place to hide.

Jael came out to meet Sisera and said to him, "Turn aside, my lord; turn aside to me; do not be afraid." So he turned aside to her into the tent, and she covered him with a rug. And he said to her, "Please give me a little water to drink, for I am thirsty." So she opened a skin of milk and gave him a drink and covered him. And he said to her, "Stand at the opening of the tent, and if any man comes and asks you, 'Is anyone here?' say, 'No.'" But Jael, the wife of Heber, took a tent peg, and took a hammer in her hand. Then she went softly to him and drove the peg into his temple until it went down into the ground while he was lying fast asleep from weariness. So he died. Judges 4:18-21.

Just as Deborah had prophesied to Barak, God had given the final victory to a woman.

There was great rejoicing in Israel. After the decisive battle, Barak went on to lead the Israelites against Jabin himself and they won. Israel was free.

Deborah was overwhelmed with joy and gratitude to God for his deliverance of his people that day and she wanted to mark the occasion.

Everyone in Israel and outside should know of God's power and might! The best way she could think to do that was with a song, much like Moses had written and sung when God rescued them at the Red Sea. A song telling of the battle and the victory could be learned and sung throughout the country, so that people would hear over and over again how great God is.

Over the next few days, Deborah and Barak worked together to craft the words and the music. You can read the entire song in Judges 5.

Deborah wanted to begin with praising God and calling all people to hear of his great works, so they wrote a song of praise to God.

That the leaders took the lead in Israel,
that the people offered themselves willingly,
bless the LORD!

Hear, O kings; give ear, O princes;
to the LORD I will sing;
I will make melody to the LORD,
the God of Israel. Judges 5:2-3.

Then they used poetry and music to tell the details of the battle and victory of God's people over the oppressor Jabin. They finished up the lengthy tale with a plea that God would punish his enemies and protect those who love and serve him.

> So may all your enemies perish, O LORD!
> But your friends be like the sun
> as he rises in his might. Judges 5:31a.

Together Deborah and Barak created a victory song that everyone in Israel heard and some even learned to sing for themselves.

JEHOSHEBA: A COURAGEOUS AUNT

2 Chronicles 21-22 & 2 Kings 11

H ave you ever watched someone do something very brave and wonder if you could ever do that? Would you have the courage to rescue someone even if it meant you might die? There is someone in the Bible who faced that question. Her name was Jehosheba.

Jehosheba was a princess. When we think of a princess we think about beautiful clothes, large houses and a lavish amount of possessions. Jehosheba had all of those things at one time in her life, but that did not mean that her life was always a happy or easy one.

In both 2 Chronicles 21 and 22 and in 2 Kings 11 we read the story of Jehosheba and her family. When Jehosheba was born at the palace in Jerusalem, her grandfather, Jehoshaphat, was King of Judah. Jehoshaphat was a good king, who loved God and obeyed his commands. And God blessed Judah during his reign. But when Jehosheba was still a young girl, her grandfather died and then her father became king.

Jehosheba's father, King Jehoram, was not a good man, nor was her mother, Queen Athalia. Neither of them worshipped God. Instead they encouraged the people to set up pagan places to worship idols and to ignore all of God's commands. And almost immediately her father ignored 'Thou shall not kill,' for he ordered his soldiers to seek out every one of his brothers and put them to death. He did this to stop any of them from trying to take the throne away from him and becoming king in his place.

Can you imagine what the palace must have been like for Jehosheba? Instead of a happy safe home, it became a place of fear and death. At that point, Jehosheba must have understood how dangerous her parents were becoming. They were willing to kill even their own family members to keep their power.

> God was angry with Jehosheba's father for his terrible deeds and told the prophet Elijah to send King Jehoram a letter saying, "Thus says the LORD, the God of David your father, 'Because you have not walked in the ways of Jehoshaphat your father, ...but.... have enticed Judah and the inhabitants of Jerusalem into whoredom, … and also you have killed your brothers, of your father's house, who were better than yourself, behold, the LORD will bring a great plague on your people, your children, your wives, and all your possessions, and you yourself will have a severe sickness with a disease of your bowels.'" 2 Chronicles 21:12b–15a.

Just think how awful it would have been to hear those words read out in the court and hear God's judgment on the king and his people. And it happened just as God said. The great plague that God brought on Judah was invasion by several armies. The soldiers from Philistia and Arabia even invaded the palace at Jerusalem. They carried off many of the treasures of the palace as well as all of Jehosheba's brothers except the youngest. Now instead of a beautiful place to live with her family, Jehosheba lived in a nearly empty palace....empty of all the beautiful furniture and decoration and empty of most of her family.

Then just as God had said, King Jehoram then became very ill. None of the doctors could cure him and he died after much suffering and pain. 'And he departed to no one's regret.' 2 Chronicles 21:20.

The people of Judah were not sorry to see him go. They knew that his disobedience had brought great trouble to their country.

But God had kept Jehosheba herself safe through all of this. And he provided her with a good husband. We are not told in the Bible exactly when Jehosheba was married, but we are told she was allowed to marry Jehoiada, a priest in God's temple. What a wonderful way God took care of Jehosheba. While the rest of her family was disobeying God, she was able to live in the temple with her husband and worship the true and living God.

After King Jehoram died, Jehosheba's brother, Ahaziah, became king. How she must have hoped that he would have learned from their father's mistakes and obey God. But he did not. Instead he listened to their mother, Athalia, who was wicked woman. She persuaded Ahaziah to keep all the pagan idols, to ignore God's commands and to make an alliance with the king of Israel who worshipped idols too.

God only allowed King Ahaziah to rule Judah for one year and then Ahaziah died. Suddenly there was great problem. Who would be the next king? All of

Ahaziah's sons were too little to be king. That was when wicked Athalia, the queen mother, decided to take the throne for herself.

Just think of the fear that Jehosheba must have felt when she heard her mother was taking all the power for herself. Jehosheba had seen her mother encourage her father to kill his own brother. She had also seen her mother tell her brother to serve idols and make wicked plans with other kings. So she knew that Queen Athalia would be a dangerous queen.

Not long after Athalia became the queen, Jehosheba heard about an awful order that her mother had given the palace soldiers.

> Now when Athaliah the mother of Ahaziah saw that her son was dead, she arose and destroyed all the royal family. 2 Kings 11:1.

Jehosheba knew she had to do something. The Bible simply says: 'But Jehosheba, the daughter of King Joram, sister of Ahaziah, took Joash the son of Ahaziah and stole him away from among the king's sons who were being put to death, and she put him and his nurse in a bedroom. Thus they hid him from Athaliah, so that he was not put to death.' 2 Kings 11:2.

In those few short words we are told that Jehosheba did something very courageous. Remember how wicked her mother, Queen Athalia, was and how she wanted to kill everyone in her family, even her grandsons? How dangerous it must have been for Jehosheba to sneak into the palace nursery just ahead of the soldiers who were coming to kill all the children.

How brave she had to be as she ran with baby Joash tight in her arms, followed by the baby's nurse, away from the palace and into the temple.

How carefully Jehosheba arranged the bedroom near her own in the temple for baby Joash and his nurse to hide.

How thankful she was to God for keeping her and the others safe in the temple, the one place her wicked mother would never visit.

God continued to keep Jehosheba, her husband, Jehoida, and the baby Joash safe for six years while Queen Athalia reigned. The wicked queen thought she had killed all her grandsons so that no one would be able to take the throne away from her. She continued to rule Judah ignoring God and thinking that God would do nothing to stop her. But God will not be mocked. A judgment was coming.

Once little Joash turned seven years old, Jehoida decided it was time to tell the captains of the guard about the boy. Joash ought to be the king, not his wicked grandmother. So Jehoida and the captains made a plan to have him crowned on a Sabbath in the temple.

He said to them 'This is the thing that you shall do: one third of you .....shall guard the palace. And the two divisions of you ... shall surround the king, each with his weapons in his hand. And whoever approaches the ranks is to be put to death. Be with the king when he goes out and when he comes in.' 2 Kings 11:5-8.

The soldiers did just as Jehoida told them the following Sabbath. A great fanfare of trumpets sounded as the crown was placed on Joash's head and then soldiers clapped their hands and shouted 'Long live the king!' When Queen Athalia heard the noise, she rushed out of the palace and over to the temple. She became very angry when she saw her young grandson standing with a crown on his head surrounded by the soldiers. And she was even angrier when she saw all the people begin to gather, rejoicing that they had a new king. She called out 'Treason!' and ordered the soldiers to stop. Instead the soldiers obeyed Jehoida and took Athalia out of the temple and put her to death along with her advisors.

Then Jehoida called all the people together and made a covenant with them and their new king to turn from their idols and serve God. The people agreed and the Bible tells us: 'Then all the people of the land went to the house of Baal and tore it down; his altars and his images they broke in pieces.... they brought the king down from the house of the LORD, marching through the gate of the guards to the king's house. And he took his seat on the throne of the kings. So all the people of the land rejoiced, and the city was quiet after Athaliah had been put to death with the sword at the king's house.' 2 Kings 11:18-20.

Joash became a good king. He listened carefully to the godly lessons Jehoida taught him as he grew up.

The Bible says: 'And Joash did what was right in the eyes of the LORD all his days, because Jehoiada the priest instructed him.' 2 Kings 12:2.

How Jehosheba must have rejoiced to see her nephew on the throne and to know that he served God. At last Judah had a good king again. But just think if Jehosheba had not been willing to rescue her nephew. What if she had not been courageous enough to sneak into the palace and run away with her baby nephew? What if she and her husband, Jehoida, had not been brave enough to keep the baby hidden and safe for six years?

God had placed Jehosheba in just the right place to carry out his plans. Jehosheba grew up in a violent family surrounded by fear and pagan beliefs. But God kept Jehosheba safe from all of that. He gave her a God fearing husband and when the time was right, he also gave her the courage to save the little baby who grew up to be a great king.

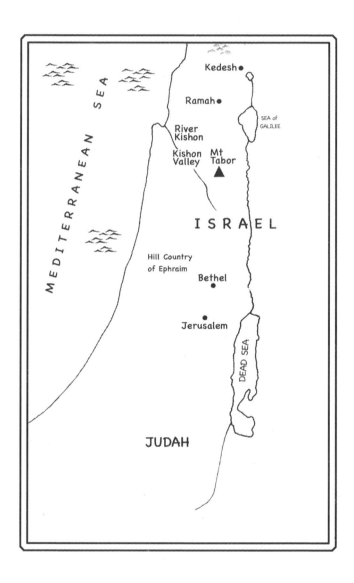

WHAT NEXT?

Y ou have now read about six women who took risks to serve God. They were all in danger because they chose to do what is right. They are a wonderful example of how to serve God even when it is difficult. You may never have to face such big dangers as they did, but each one of us who serves God and speaks out for what is right takes a risk. We risk people laughing at us or making life difficult for us. But just as these women trusted God to help them, even when they were afraid, so we can trust God to help us. He has promised never to leave us or forsake us. When we call on him he will answer. Are you ready to take the risk of following God? Even if none of your friends or family do? God has promised us great blessing when we serve him as we should.

RISKTAKER QUIZ

Katherine von Bora

1. When was Katherine von Bora born?

2. What country was she born in?

3. When Katherine and the other nuns escaped from the convent what else was in the wagon?

4. What was the name of the man who helped them escape from the convent?

5. What was the name of the town where Martin Luther lived?

RISKTAKER QUIZ

Fidelia Fiske

1. In which U.S. state was Fidelia Fiske born?

2. What disease did Fidelia suffer from when she was younger?

3. What is the land of Persia now called?

4. What Psalm was sung during the funeral?

5. What was the name given to the mob who attacked the school?

RISKTAKER QUIZ

Amy Carmichael

1. Where was Amy born?

2. Who did Amy hear speaking at the Keswick convention and what happened to her there?

3. Where did Amy go to first as a missionary?

4. What was the name of the book that was used to teach the village women about Jesus?

5. Why was Amy given the name Amma by the orphans?

RISKTAKER QUIZ

Lillian Dickson

1. Where was Lillian born?

2. Why did the Dicksons have to leave Formosa?

3. What did Lillian and Eugenia bring with them on their journey?

4. What dangerous thing did Hui-ben tell Lillian was coming?

5. When Eugenia asked the villagers if they wanted to learn about health and nutrition what did they say?

RISKTAKER QUIZ

Deborah

1. In Deborah's time there were no kings in Israel. Who did God appoint to rule the land instead?

2. Under what type of tree did Deborah sit?

3. Why did God allow Jabin to invade the land of Israel?

4. Who did Barak want to go with him into battle?

5. What weather conditions did God use to help Deborah and the Israelites defeat their enemies?

RISKTAKER QUIZ

Jehosheba

1. What were the names of Jehosheba's parents?

2. Who did King Ahaziah listen to?

3. What did Athalia want to do to her grandson?

4. For how long did Jehosheba and Jehoida hide Joash?

5. When Athalia heard the people shout, 'Long live the King!' what did she call out?

RISKTAKER QUIZ
ANSWERS

KATHERINE VON BORA
1. 1499
2. Germany
3. Fish barrels
4. Mr Koppe
5. Wittenberg

FIDELIA FISKE
1. Massachusetts
2. Typhoid
3. Iran
4. Psalm 46
5. The Nestorians

AMY CARMICHAEL
1. Millisle, Northern Ireland
2. Hudson Taylor; She was converted or trusted in Jesus Christ to save her from her sins
3. Japan
4. The Wordless book
5. Amma is the Tamil name for mother

LILLIAN DICKSON
1. Prior Lake, Minnesota
2. The Second World War
3. Flannelgraph stories and medical supplies
4. A typhoon
5. They wanted to hear about God instead

DEBORAH
1. Judges
2. A Palm tree
3. As a punishment. The people of Israel had disobeyed God
4. Deborah
5. Rain and mud

JEHOSHEBA
1. King Jehoram and Queen Athalia
2. Athalia, his mother
3. Kill him
4. Six years
5. Treason

GLOSSARY

Abbess – The female superior of an abbey of nuns

Caste – Many countries operate a caste system, including India. It is a social group that determines what jobs you can do, who you can marry and what influence you may have in your country

Cells – A sleeping room only big enough to hold a bed and a small storage chest

Cloister – A covered walkway which is open on one side and runs along the side of a building that faces a quadrangle. Often found in religious buildings

Compline – Prayers at the end of the day

Convent or Nunnery – A convent is a community of nuns or the building used to house them. It is particularly used by the Roman Catholic church

Doctrine – A collection of beliefs or instructions. Christian Doctrine is the truths that the Bible teaches; the teaching and explanation of the Word of God

Excommunication – This happens when the religious leaders decide that a person is teaching false doctrine and should no longer be allowed to be part of a religious community or church. During Martin Luther's time an excommunicated person wasn't allowed to attend church, conduct any type of business or even buy food or clothing. Anyone who helped an excommunicated person could be punished

Hindu - This is the most common religion in India. Its followers worship a variety of false gods. Without the saving knowledge of Jesus Christ they believe that in order to get to heaven they must live a good life. However, the Bible tells us that our good works are never good enough to save us - it is only through the Lord Jesus Christ that we can be saved.

Infirmaress - The nun in charge of the hospital

Nestorian - A group of people who do not believe that Jesus Christ was both God and man

Nun - A woman who has taken special vows committing her to a religious life

Pope - The man in charge of the Roman Catholic Church

Refectory - The dining hall in a convent

Sari - A female garment from the Indian sub-continent. A strip of unstitched cloth several metres in length. It is wound around the body in a variety of styles

Seminary - A theological or Christian college or university

Shah - Another name for the king of Persia

Typhoon - A tropical storm or cyclone that forms in the North West Pacific Ocean

Vespers - A late afternoon or evening prayer service

WHO IS LINDA FINLAYSON?

Linda Finlayson is a Canadian living in the USA in the area of Philadelphia. She has enjoyed working with children in schools, churches and children's clubs. Bringing together her love of books, children and history has given her the opportunity to write the adventure stories of real people.

Linda is married and has one son. She has also written *Wilfred Grenfell: Arctic Adventurer.*

ADVENTURE AND FAITH

Linda Finlayson has written another book with stories of adventure and faith where we read about different men who took risks and faced dangerous situations for the glory of God.

Martin Luther stood up for the truth and was kidnapped, David Brainerd trekked through unchartered territories to preach the Gospel, William King sacrificed his own wealth for the freedom of others, Brother Andrew risked his life to smuggle Bibles into Communist countries. Nehemiah took a stand in order to rebuild the walls of Jerusalem and Stephen spoke the truth even though it meant he lost his life.

These are the stories of real men who took real risks for God.

ISBN: 978-1-84550-491-5

CHRISTIAN FOCUS PUBLICATIONS

Christian Christian CF4K Mentor
Focus Heritage

Christian Focus Publications publishes books for adults and children under its four main imprints: Christian Focus, Christian Heritage, CF4K and Mentor. Our books reflect that God's word is reliable and Jesus is the way to know him, and live for ever with him.

Our children's publication list includes a Sunday school curriculum that covers pre-school to early teens; puzzle and activity books. We also publish personal and family devotional titles, biographies and inspirational stories that children will love.

If you are looking for quality Bible teaching for children then we have an excellent range of Bible story and age specific theological books. From pre-school to teenage fiction, we have it covered!

Find us at our web page:
www.christianfocus.com